Written by Jocelyn Hubbell
Illustrated by Jean Cassels

Reviewed by Frank Indiviglio, Zoologist,
Wildlife Conservation Society, New York.

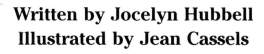

© 2000 McClanahan Book Company, Inc.
All rights reserved.
Published by McClanahan Book Company, Inc.
A Division of Learning Horizons
1 American Road, Cleveland OH 44144
ISBN: 0-7681-0230-8
Printed in the U.S.A.
10 9 8 7 6 5 4 3 2 1

There are at least 4,000 different kinds of frogs in the world. They live on all the continents except Antarctica, and they've been around since the time of the dinosaurs.

Most frogs live near ponds, lakes, and swamps—but not all of them. Some live in deserts, others in jungles, and some even survive in the cold Arctic!

But just what are frogs?
(Hint: turn the page to find out...)

Frogs are...

amphibians (am-FIB-ee-enz). And all amphibians are **ectothermic**—or cold-blooded—which means their body temperature is the same as the temperature around them. To warm up, frogs sunbathe in moist places where their skin will stay in top condition—wet and slimy!

Bullfrog

Most frogs have smooth, moist skin. They do not have feathers, fur, or scales.

Green Frog

The word *amphibian* means "with two lives." Most baby frogs live in the water and look nothing like the adults that live on land. (Turn the page to find out how frogs make this amazing leap from one life to another.)

How do Frogs Grow up?

A frog's body undergoes some astounding changes before it becomes an adult. This is called **metamorphosis** (met-uh-MOR-foh-sis). It has three steps.

1. Eggs

Frogs begin their life as soft, jelly-like eggs. Most adult female frogs lay their eggs in water. They place their eggs where the babies will be able to find food and hide from hungry **predators** such as birds, fishes, and turtles.

eggs

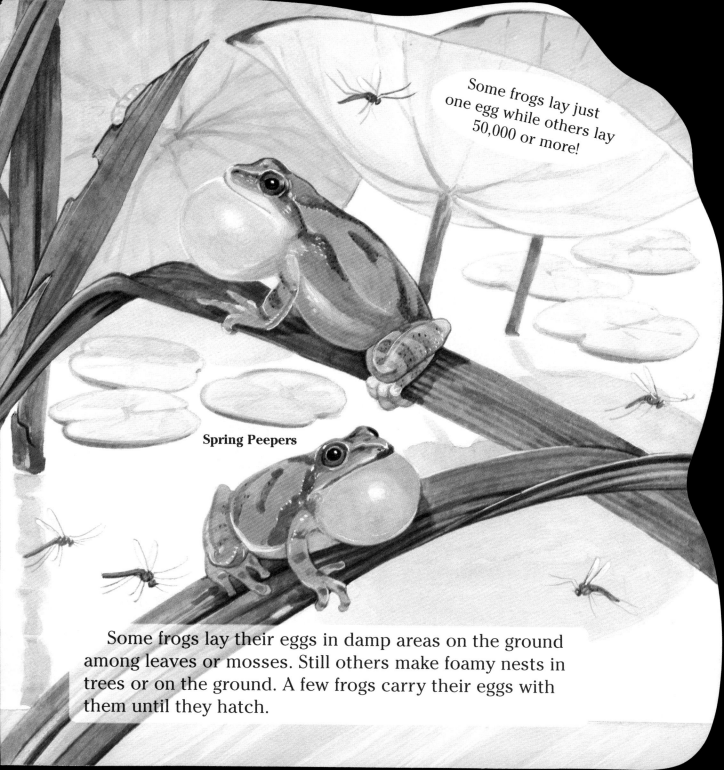

Some frogs lay just one egg while others lay 50,000 or more!

Spring Peepers

Some frogs lay their eggs in damp areas on the ground among leaves or mosses. Still others make foamy nests in trees or on the ground. A few frogs carry their eggs with them until they hatch.

2. Tadpoles

After several days to several weeks, **larvae** hatch from the eggs. Larvae are also called tadpoles. They have large, round heads and long, slender tails for quick swimming. They breathe underwater with **gills** just as fish do.

tadpoles

Most tadpoles are plant eaters, or **herbivores**. They filter out small particles of plant material in the water, or scrape at vegetation with their tiny teeth. Some tadpoles are meat eaters, or **carnivores**. They eat tiny insects, animals, and other frogs' eggs!

As tadpoles grow, internal gills take the place of their external gills. Within a few months they grow hind legs, then front legs. Their tails slowly shorten. Then their eyes and mouths become larger.

Some frogs do not have a tadpole stage. They hatch from eggs as tiny **froglets**.

Tadpoles also begin to grow lungs. They swim to the water's surface to test their lungs by gulping air.

3. Adults

After two to four months, most tadpoles are ready to become adult frogs. The adults no longer have gills. Like you, they breathe through lungs.

Using long, powerful hind legs and webbed feet, the adults can now walk, hop or jump on land, and swim in water. There are even frogs that can climb trees.

Bullfrog

Green Frog

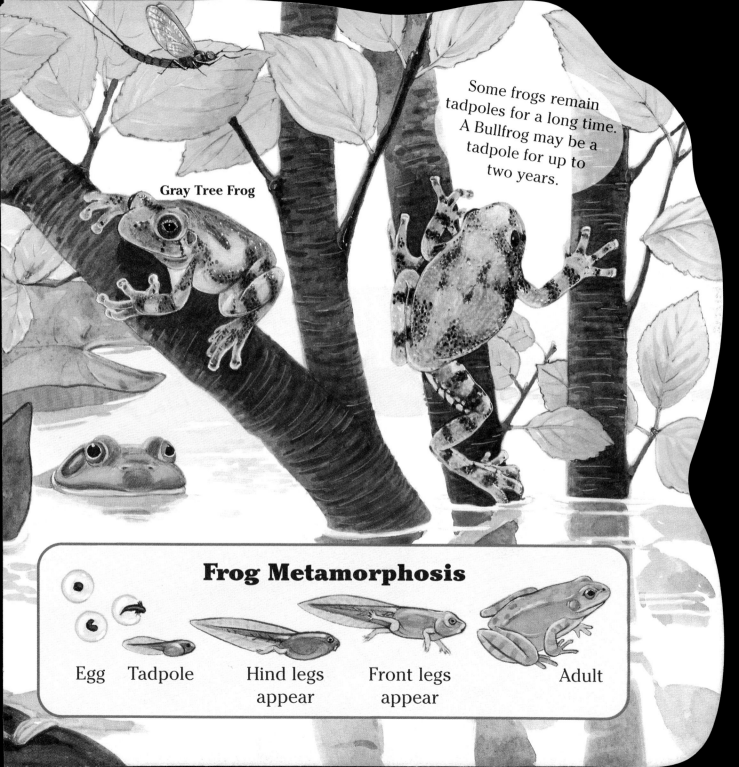

Gray Tree Frog

Some frogs remain tadpoles for a long time. A Bullfrog may be a tadpole for up to two years.

Frog Metamorphosis

Egg Tadpole Hind legs appear Front legs appear Adult

Why are Frogs so Slimy?

Some frogs have special glands in their skin that produce **mucous**—that's the stuff that makes frogs feel slimy! Others produce a waxy substance to keep their bodies from losing water and drying out. A frog will die if it doesn't keep its skin moist.

As a frog grows, it has to shed its skin. This is called **molting**. The frog pulls off its old skin with its feet—then eats it!

Tree frogs have sticky mucous glands on their toes that help them climb.

When molting, the old
skin splits down the back.

Then the frog uses its hind
legs to push the skin over its
head and into its mouth.

Bullfrog

Believe it or not, scientist
have developed many life-saving
medicines from the chemicals
in frogs' skin!

You have to see it to eat it!

Frogs see things best from a distance of 2 to 20 feet (0.6–6 m) away. Up close, a fly could hide right in front of a frog's nose!

Frog's eyes do more that just see. They also help a frog swallow its food! When a frog has taken in a large mouthful, it pulls its eyes into the roof of its mouth to help push the food down its throat.

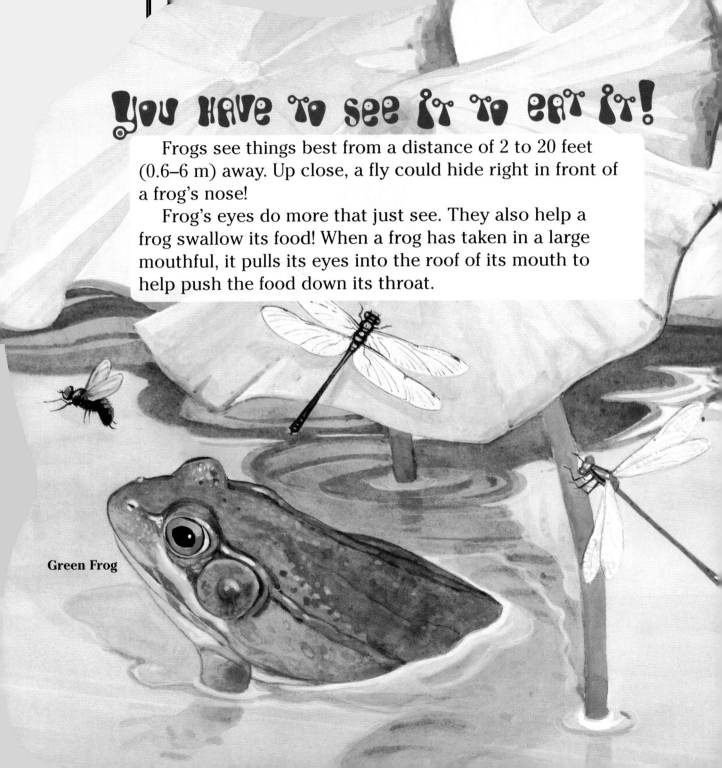

Green Frog

A frog can see in all directions with its bulging, high-set eyes.

A frog's ears are called tympanums (tim-PA-numz). Frogs can hear very well.

Bullfrog

Many frogs use their sense of smell to guide them back to the ponds where they were born to lay their own eggs.

How do frogs eat?

Most frogs have big mouths and long, sticky tongues. They flick out their tongues—**SLURP**—to catch their **prey**. Frogs have small, sharp teeth that tightly hold the prey so it cannot escape as it is being swallowed whole!

One frog can eat up to 10,000 insects in one summer!

Northern Leopard Frog

Big-mouthed Bullfrogs eat insects, birds, fish, mice, snakes, small turtles, and even other frogs.

Most frogs hunt at night and eat insects. Many of them also eat spiders, snails, slugs, worms, crayfish and other small animals. They catch larger prey with their mouth or front feet.

Staying Alive!

Frogs have to be able to hide or run from predators. They must also survive extreme temperatures and periods without food.

Poison Arrow Frogs

Bright colors warn predators that a frog is poisonous.

The African bullfrog can give predators a sharp, painful bite!

Wood Frogs and Gray Treefrogs can survive the winter because their bodies produce a natural antifreeze!

Flying frogs can leap out of trees and glide using their large webbed feet as parachutes.

Some frogs puff up their bodies to look bigger when facing a predator.

Many frogs dig into the ground to escape long periods of heat and dryness. Other frogs may sleep through winter buried in mud at the bottom of a pond until spring.

Toad or Frog?

Actually, all toads are frogs. Toads share certain characteristics with frogs and also have some unique ones of their own.

Frogs have:

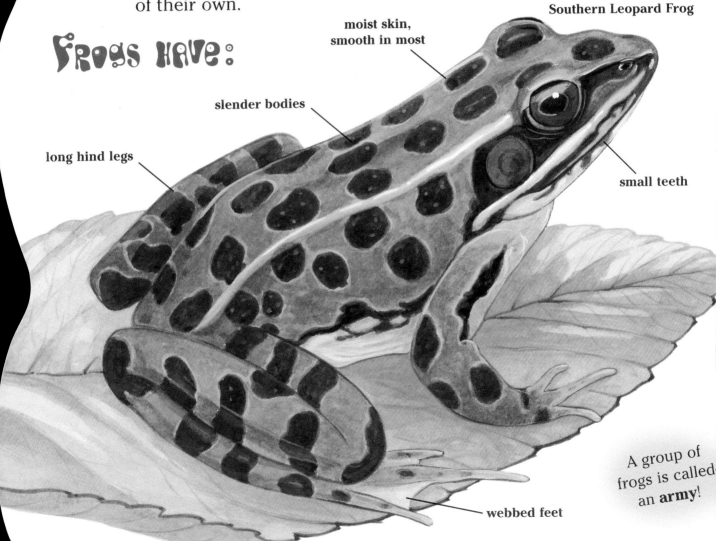

Southern Leopard Frog

moist skin, smooth in most

slender bodies

long hind legs

small teeth

webbed feet

A group of frogs is called an **army**!

Toads have:

American Toad

poison glands behind eyes

dry skin, bumpy in most

short, plump bodies

no teeth

short hind legs

feet have little webbing

And you can find these amazing amphibians . . .